WITH

PING-PONG
BALLS

By Eiji Orii and Masako Orii   Pictures by Kimimaro Yoshida

Gareth Stevens Children's Books
Milwaukee

Library of Congress Cataloging-in-Publication Data

Orii, Eiji, 1909-
   Simple science experiments with ping-pong balls.

   (Simple science experiments)
   Includes index.
   1. Air—Experiments—Juvenile literature.
I. Orii, Masako. II. Title. III. Series.
QC161.2.075   1988   533'.6   88-22508
ISBN 1-55532-852-0

North American edition first published in 1989 by

Gareth Stevens Children's Books
7317 West Green Tree Road
Milwaukee, Wisconsin 53223, USA

This US edition copyright ©1989. First published as *Odoru Pinpondama (Let's Try Ping Pong Balls)* in Japan with an original copyright © 1988 by Eiji Orii, Masako Orii, and Kimimaro Yoshida. English translation rights arranged with Dainippon-Tosho Publishing Co., Ltd., through Japan Foreign-Rights Centre, Tokyo.

Additional text and illustrations copyright © 1989 by Gareth Stevens, Inc.

Series editor and additional text: Rita Reitci
Research editor: Scott Enk
Additional illustrations: John Stroh
Design: Laurie Shock
Translated from the Japanese by Jun Amano
Technical consultant: Jonathan Knopp, Chair, Science Department, Rufus King High School, Milwaukee

1 2 3 4 5 6 7 8 9 94 93 92 91 90 89

What is nearly as light as air — and can help us find out some things air can do? Ping-pong balls!

Paper, apples, kitchen funnels, soda bottles, and some other things will also help us learn about air currents and how they can change the pressure of air.

Be ready for some surprises as you discover the tricks air can play!

See if your breath will go through glass. Ask a grown-up to help you light a candle and cover it with a drinking glass. Then quickly cover the glass with a handkerchief or a piece of cloth.

Now blow at the covered glass. What happens?

Look — the candle is out!

Let's try it again. This time wait about half a minute before you cover the glass. The candle goes out before you blow at the glass.

Your breath really does not go through glass, does it? The candle flame uses up all the oxygen inside the glass and so the flame dies out.

Place a soda bottle in front of a lighted candle. Blow at the bottle. Why does the candle go out? The air you blow at the bottle follows the curve around each side. When the streams of air meet at the back, they blow out the flame.

Now try it with something wider than the soda bottle.

How about an apple? This works best with a large apple.
Place a candle behind the apple about 2 inches (5 cm)
away and light it. What happens if you blow at the apple?

The flame goes out.

When a stream of air moves fast, it pushes less strongly to its sides. We say that the air pressure of this stream is lower. The normal air pressure in the room then pushes your breath against the sides of the apple so that it follows the curve.

Do it again, but this time place the lighted candle farther behind the apple. What happens now?

The flame flickers but does not go out.

The air current from your breath weakens the farther it travels.

Ask an adult to cut the apple in half. Place it before the lighted candle with the cut part toward you. Now blow. Where does the air flow this time?

Some shapes help air flow around them. Different shapes make air flow in other directions.

Cut a square out of a thick piece of cardboard. Hold two of the points lightly between your finger and thumb and blow gently at the square.

Where does the square point?

Wind pushes against the weather vane, first on one side, then on the other, as it tries to turn away. This keeps the thin edge into the wind. So the weather vane points in the direction the wind is blowing.

The candle flames heat the air. The hot air rises and spins the propeller blades that turn the angels around and around.

Place a postcard on a table. Hold a glass or plastic funnel upside down close over the postcard.

What happens if you suck through the funnel?

What happens if you blow through the funnel?

If you suck real hard . . . the postcard will come up from the table.

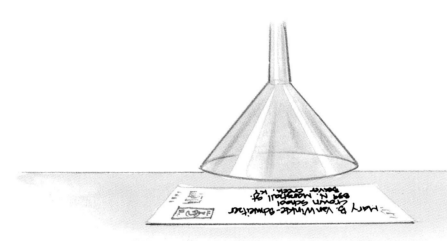

If you blow . . . the postcard still comes up!

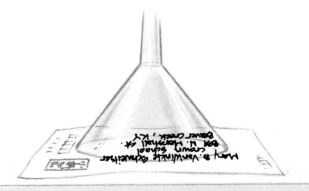

Both blowing and sucking lower the air pressure on top of the postcard. The normal air pressure in the room then pushes the postcard toward the lower pressure that you make inside the funnel.

Hold a ping-pong ball up inside a funnel. Bend over so that the large opening of the funnel is over the floor or a table. Now blow hard into the funnel and let go of the ping-pong ball. What happens?

The ping-pong ball does not fall. Does blowing lower the air pressure inside the funnel? Does the pressure of the surrounding air keep the ball from falling?

Put a penny or a dime inside the funnel and cover the smaller opening with your finger. Now blow hard at the coin. What happens?

The coin comes up. How does blowing at the coin make it move upward?

Try it again. This time do not cover the small opening. Now air rushes in from the bottom. The air pressure stays the same. The coin stays inside.

Place a postage stamp on a desk. Hold a coin about half an inch (1 cm) above the stamp. See what happens when you blow on top of the coin.

Put one paper cup loosely inside another. Blow into the space between the cups. What happens?

Place two ping-pong balls close together on a table. Aim a drinking straw between them and blow gently. What happens to the balls?

The balls come closer together.

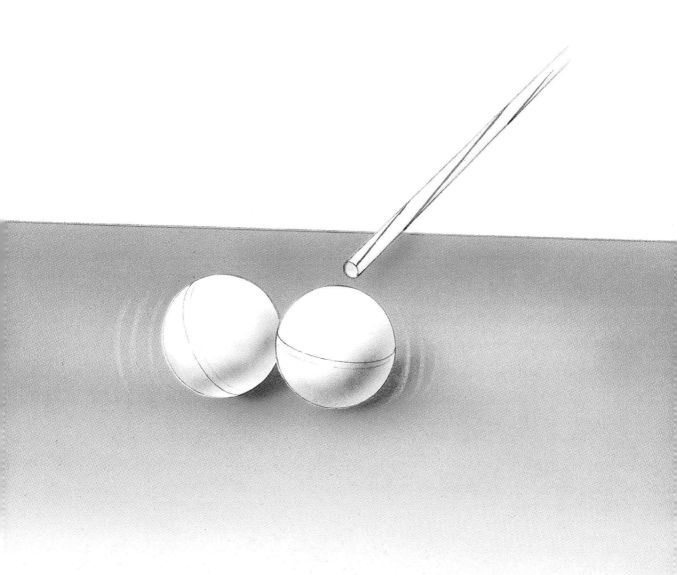

The fast-moving stream of air lowers the air pressure between the balls, and they come toward each other.

Cut two rectangles the same size out of paper. Now hold them just below the level of your chin and blow down between them. What happens?

Hold one of your paper rectangles as shown. What happens when you blow air across the paper?

The fast-moving air on the top of the paper has lower pressure. The normal air pressure underneath pushes the paper upward. This is how wings keep an airplane up as it flies.

Try to take the ping-pong ball out of the glass without using your hands.

Remember, no hands!

Blow air into the glass.

Lay an empty soda bottle on a table with the neck just over the edge. Crumple up a small piece of paper and put it about 1 inch (2 cm) into the bottle's neck so that it is very loose.

Can you get the paper out without touching the bottle?

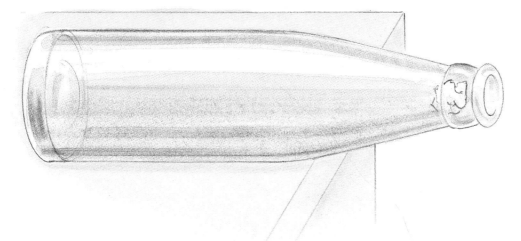

Blow air into the bottle. Now blow air across the bottle's mouth.

Put a drinking straw in your mouth and look upward. Hold a ping-pong ball over the end of the straw. Now let go of the ball while blowing air through the straw. What happens?

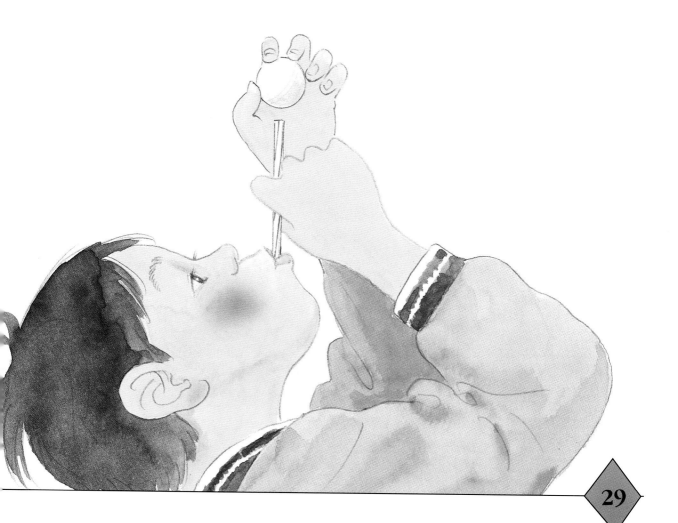

Ask a grown-up to help you take the nozzle off the garden hose. Turn on the water gently and hold the end of the hose straight up. Now place a ping-pong ball on the water. What happens? You may have to turn the water up or down to make the ping-pong ball dance.

Tape a thread to a ping-pong ball. Turn on a faucet. Holding the thread, bring the ball close to the water. What happens?

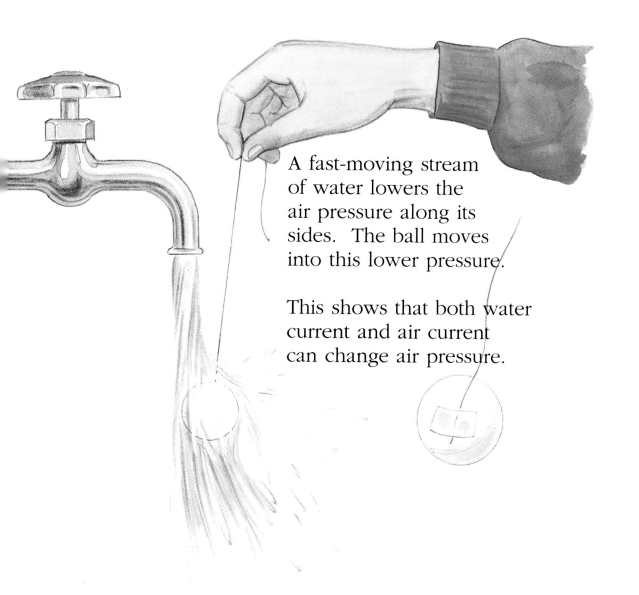

A fast-moving stream of water lowers the air pressure along its sides. The ball moves into this lower pressure.

This shows that both water current and air current can change air pressure.

GLOSSARY

Here is a list of words and phrases used in this book. After you read what each word or phrase means, you can see it used in a sentence.

air current: a flow of air
They felt an air current in the cave.

air pressure: the weight of air. Higher air pressure means the air is heavier than normal; lower air pressure means it is lighter than normal.
The air pressure at sea level is normally about 15 pounds per square inch.

funnel: a cone with a tube at the small end, for pouring liquids into containers
He poured gas through a funnel into the lawn mower tank.

nozzle: a spout at the end of a hose to control the flow of water
He tightened the nozzle to get a fine spray of water.

oxygen: the most important gas in the air, needed by most living things in order to live
A fire must have oxygen in order to burn.

ping-pong ball: a table tennis ball, named for the sounds the ball makes when hit by a paddle
He hits the ping-pong ball much too hard.

postcard: a rectangle 3 x 6 inches (8 x 15 cm) of light cardboard with space for an address on one side and a written message on the other
My uncle sent me a postcard from Denver, Colorado.

propeller: two or more blades of metal, twisted so as to rotate in air or water
My cousin flies an airplane with a single propeller.

weather vane: a flat piece of metal that swings in the wind in order to show the direction from which the wind is blowing
A weather vane is often made in the shape of an animal, like a horse or a rooster.

INDEX